THE WHITE SHIRTS OF SUMMER

THE WHITE SHIRTS OF SUMMER

New and Selected Poems

Mamang Dai

SPEAKING
TIGER

SPEAKING TIGER BOOKS LLP
125A, Ground Floor, Shahpur Jat, near Asiad Village,
New Delhi 110049

First published by Speaking Tiger in 2023

ISBN: 978-93-5447-637-2
eISBN: 978-93-5447-639-6

10 9 8 7 6 5 4 3 2 1

Typeset in ArnhemFine by SÜRYA, New Delhi
Printed at Shree Maitrey Printech Pvt. Ltd., Noida

The wild geese
Do not intend to cast their reflection;
The water has no mind
To receive their image.

—Haiku from *Zenrin-kushū*
(*Anthology of Passages from the Forest of Zen*)

CONTENTS

Songbird

How sad it is, remembrance.
The warm sweat of the seasons
the narrow boats of grief
a white moon;
my dream of a songbird
a songbird in the garden.

When We Needed Someone

When we needed someone
I cried for the shaman,
seeking the words of generations to accompany us.
Where are all the shamans?

We needed someone
to mend these bones, lift this arm,
dress this shoulder, spine, collar, with fine ornaments
and place a spell under these feet
to heal this heart
and reclaim life and splendour.

The strong, black beetle is an uncle
visiting on the back of the wind
this rainy morning.
No, words are not dead—
rustling through the trees
the shamans are in the garden,
their craft is not ended,
recounting each weathered moment
like beads in a long conversation
to win mastery over time.

We meet here every day—
shamans, prayers, spirits.
The bees bring me a message:
This is for your protection,
remember, and believe
the truth about land—
rainwater, sleep.

The truth about love—
eating flowers and thorns.

The truth about life—
eating flowers and thorns.

Long Pining

Long pining river. River,
wear emerald, it's your colour.
Time may turn black sometimes
like this night, dying, dying,
wear firelight for your hair
and an earring of teardrops
glistening in the air.

In the east the sun is travelling
fast, so fast—
one day it is wild grass,
then lilies and oleander,
brown earth, rain and roses
mixed together.

The Tree with a Thousand Flowers

The tree with a thousand flowers
is shining outside my window.
The sky is a shell,
on the wave of a pearl grey mist
a mermaid is weeping over the hills,
so far away from the sea.

The voices of men and women echo out of corners.
The rain is trying to transform some sad absence
into the patience of green.

Is faith greater than hope?
What will happen to the broken twig,
will it mend?
My willow wand is a wavering line
written in sand.
Unable to decipher where words spring from
I stare and stare at the rain
burnishing everything anew.

Once Upon a Time in Pasighat

(For friends of a different sort)

The house is unswept
Never mind whoever comes
Bamboo leaves scraping the floor;
My friends are of a different sort.

If you see a fly
Do not lift your white hand, my love,
The cobweb in the corner
Will do the job,

And if the town lights die
We'll sit with the wind
Inside, outside;
My friends are of a different sort.

Each star has its soul
In your sleeping eyes, my love,
Dreams will rise and fall
Slowly coming to rest.

When the house grows old
Tomorrow, our children will know

Timelessness
With friends of their sort

Under the broad roof:
Slanting beams of light,
The beauty of bone,
The universe on the walls.

Hello, Mountain

Every morning when the forest wakes
The canopy goes for a walk
Hailing the sun, courting the wind
Discussing fruit and weather

The idle moss turns into velvet
Branches make signs.
Who says there is no time?
The only thing we are given is Time.

Chattering life high above,
Babel of tree dwellers.
For a seed falling so far down
To rise again, time is a given.
A foothold for the hunger of a weed,
Colour, scent, camouflage
And the grass that never sleeps

Shooting up to meet the gaze of the mountain.
How are you, mountain?
Is everything all right?
Is the earth growing old,
Birds flying away, trees falling?

Green Mountain wearing a rain hat,
Are there caves and bats in your bosom,
Wedged in your folds
A hum of voices celebrating
The anniversaries of birth and time?
Is a raindrop growing into a river,
A rock into a jewel?

Mad Poet

The shining hammer of rain
is knocking down roads and mountains.
Come away, mad poet lolling by the door,
come away—

there is no time to say anything properly.
Flooded with images
the world is a pounding sphere
teaching love, teaching hate,
the man who loved flowers died
with a red band around his neck.

Pick up your gun, take that knife,
fix that face of yours—
mad poet, twilight breeze
tugging at your sleeve.
Once, it happened; we let a loved one die
by our absence.
Now he cannot leave,
held by the eternity of a woman's smile
when someone wrote about Time
and the happiness of young mothers
with their children.

It is no use pretending
that we have changed identity.
Tossed on the waves
the boats of summer are slipping away
into the future.
Azalea, azalea, bursting with love,
clinging to cliff and rock.
Is this a suitable place?
Why not—

rain falling down on his head,
mad concoction of air and water,
mad poet lolling by the door,
dreaming the whirling hum of moments
feeding black earth and empty space
this summer night,
simple again, in the solace of the years,
humming with the circular hum of time.

NB—2014

Who does not know
that the unhappy woman will live forever.
Come, I will tell you a story.
There was a woman who only thought of death
because her heart was heavy.
A black wind surrounded her,
her eyes were dead.
Come, there is a way out.
Who does not know the wind is a traveller
blowing into an invisible world
resonant with magic.

Your children will grow up,
a wild boy, an enchanted girl.
Your words will pave the way
chanting mysteries no one understands.
When they believe, the words will come true.

Do not doubt that the unhappy woman
can mediate with gods,
having tasted salt, the blood of tigers,
wounded flesh, alive with thoughts of death
demanding of a god a new life.
Who else can claim such a wish?
Everyone knows
the unhappy woman lives forever.

In Memoriam

In the past many things happened.
It rained, and we plunged into the river,
our hearts in our mouths,
ready to turn into a current.

Time was a river
wearing a headdress of ice.
A flashing summer
with the face of the long cloud
camouflaged with light,
bending low,
when a small town suddenly fell asleep
as the sun dipped down
one afternoon.

Stronger than illness or injury
I thought we would grow old together.
How can it be that we will not visit
those winding places wet with rain,
when there is more to find out
about freedom and love.

In secret we dreamt of new beginnings,
of work we would do.
Who knows—

Time is a narrative of finding words,
losing them,
to find them again in another place,
waiting with the wind and stars
in the mountains where we were born,
for the short walk together
to retrieve those stones with names:
Adi Pasi, Siang, Wakro, Liromoba.

Ago Goram

(April, Burial Ground)

There is warmth in the small shed
slanting west.
The earth is clean, red with mineral,
and the invisible worm and ants
are all doing their thing—
comrades of the long sleep.

Every morning the wild cinnamon
throws down a few leaves—
There!
The words we seek
have turned into green fruit.
The rose of a distant morning knows
Her time is over.
Let June, July,
midsummer do the rest.

Green Jacket

Bird on a branch
Song of life
The dancing heart—
I too have known many things.
What is it that I have not known?

What I don't know:

It's about a green jacket.
My father has been wearing it
since the day he stood on the tarmac
and waved goodbye to mum
on her way to hospital.

It's been a year now.
Don't you want to take it off,
feel the warm breeze?
The lilies are turning towards the sun.

Muffled breath,
shuffling out into the garden,
his hands are hidden,
pockets bulging with love.
When mum died, he clutched the green jacket
and sang songs of the village,
festival songs of travel and light.

Maybe he is a shaman.
His hands are shaking the yoksa,
ancient sword-blade of songs
rising out of stones and tears.
When a sunbird appeared, circling the garden,
all those who saw it exclaimed
it was the soul of the departed.

Who knows, maybe souls
sing to one another.

Benevolent earth, compassionate earth,
hidden in the folds of cloth
a jackfruit is growing in the colour green.
When there is no word for time
but for the stretching slope of the seasons
and the way a flower begins to droop
after 2 o'clock in the afternoon.

In this fleeting territory
the cloth belongs to the wearer,
bundled up with these verses:
Death of a river, a glimpse of hope,
the length of a rope, the sleeve of a jacket
to climb up to the stars.

No Turning Back

ICU.
The eager doctor is always waiting,
tap-tapping.
Now for a diagnostic tap:
Hold your breath, mother,
the clock is ticking.

We were thinking of returning,
the route you outlined
fixed in our minds.
Wait, wait,
it may take some time
but we'll reach home yet.
It is what we said.

Is that the nurse
lurking by the door, by the door
the machine with the long tube
pounding in her head?
Hold your breath, mother,
there's havoc in the air.

The hunter's needle is stalking
veins and cells.
The bent cannula is leaking,

dripping into towels
and fluids gathered around your head.

Here is a demonstration
laid out on the bed.
My mother's blood roars like a river.
Someone should shout
STOP! THAT'S ENOUGH!
GET OUT.
Clear the room for light and space.
But the man on a peacock chariot
is already on his way, driving up a storm.
Why did we delay?

In another garden a bird is wheeling free,
radiating indescribable colour.
A green grasshopper climbs up on my shoulder.
Hold your breath, mother,
The children are going to bed.

No Turning Back (2)

There is no turning back.
After this break it is all over.
Our roads are separate, our boats different,
even in dreams, thunder and lightning,
there is no return.

Then what are these songs
echoing up and down the river
with eager young men feeling
at the centre of an adventure,
shooting the breeze?

Maybe she is travelling in peace,
says the old man,
dreaming a dream of my mother
crossing the northern mountains.

Strange map, this,
piled up with all the old things.
All the different parts of us
remembering different things,
from here—to there—
this house, garden, hill,
testing memory's skill.
Even now the sunlight rests,
haunted, on the window sill.

Palindrome

My father spared us the hospital visits.
He didn't say much, as if it would confuse us
if he said he was not hungry,
or that he was too tired to walk to the gate.

Sometimes I heard him singing in his room.
I am comfortable here, he said,
all wrapped up, heater on.
When you grow old everything catches up
as if on cue—hair, sight, sound, limbs,
even the night lamp flickers, retreating
into shrinking space,
living like a guest in your own house.

If you had stayed a little longer
sunlight was spreading across the garden.
We could have thrown off our caps and jackets
and basked in the sun like iguanas.
Or simply stayed still
like resident geckos entranced in the moment
looking at the green mountain.

When old people die,
everyone says it is a matter of time.
It is the way good men should go, peacefully
in their own home, asleep in their beds.

What do you say, February moon,
What do you say?

Never in a thousand years
will we see another day like this.
Never will we feel this shipwreck
of survivors in a strange space:
The bed, the chair,
the door to the bathroom, tap dripping.

Now we'll never know what old men wait for,
waiting quietly and for so long,
since we were small and they were young
perhaps waiting for this moment,
praying to find us ready
when we turn to look
and find the green mountain is gone.

Locked Down, August 2019

He saw the small, puffy cloud on the first day. It was creeping up behind the hill directly in line with his gaze as he sat in his room doing nothing.

Yes, yes, there was a book open on the table, but he was doing nothing, just waiting. Like an entire people locked down in Paradise, waiting.

Oh, the difference between understanding and non-understanding.... He had read that somewhere. Was it in that open book? No, no, he had read it a long time ago and the lines had stuck.

Oh oh oh, it was hot. He pondered the Amazon fires. The news made out as if the planet was on fire. Maybe it was.

The puff ball of a cloud had disappeared. Rainmaker, rainmaker, make some rain.

The face of an old man passed before his eyes. It was Homer! Alive for thousands of years, waiting for rain in a desert cave. He'd read that somewhere too. Another book.

Now the sky was spotless again. He didn't like that blank space. It made his stomach churn. A buzzing jolted him. A cicada was hanging upside down on the curtain. He shook the curtain violently. Zzzt! the cicada fell to the floor. He grabbed it and flung it out through the window.

Soon we'll have an invasion of insects, the way our forests are dying, and everything running to find a place somewhere. Somewhere else. Before that too would change—a place to run from.

Ants were eating his door posts. Every day he swept away a dark clump. It made them regroup and return overnight—black, invincible.

He remembered a story from his childhood. Someone shot a stag gambolling in the Milky Way. Shot it with an arrow. The wounded stag fell and landed on the rack above the fireplace. Hah, now hear this. The man had a stack of racks for preserving food—meat, grain, fish, condiments—imagine! Always shoring up for hard times. The stag jumped up from his fall on the upper rack and the man hunted him down to the lower rack and then the one below—from the *perap* to the *rammong* to the *merom* fireplace, but the stag eluded him and scrambled out of the house into the forest.

The man leapt after him and so, man and stag have been running in this wild hunting game of search and find, find food, find shelter, a patch of earth, a tree, a branch, a woman by the stream, a field on a hill, a fortress of stone and rock.

This waiting. Waiting. And all this time not a drop of rain has touched his lips. No water has slaked his thirst. Instead, sweat runs off his body like rivulets. Full of salt.

Did he have a fever?

No one came to visit. *Let him be*—he knew they said that. *He loves solitude.* So, nothing and no one arrived. He thumped his chest.

The desolation of peace.... A poet had said that. Where had he read it?

There are ways and ways of saying things. There is rain, and summer, and last year and the year before. We are sailing, sailing, thinking we know something.

He dreamt of a cascade of words filling hill and valley. Such a volley of words, who could resist such words of love and light?

High in the mountains a harvest of walnuts is spread out to dry. The broken shells are like pellets. The sun is a burning god. Oh! Red August, red, red, many-armed season of deception and unrest. A harvest of lies is piling up like daggers. One day the knives will have a life of their own.

What is the news this burning afternoon?

He peered out. The cicadas were tuning up. Strum. Strum. Twang. Twang.

Already the small birds of morning were testing the strength of a twig, dancing in the big, patient trees. No summer rest for them. And so, they would accomplish everything in their life span.

Lockdown

We were born green
cocooned in the rituals of growing things
planting, preparing auspicious symbols for a New Year
when the sickle of time cut everything down
and the thermal guns were out.

1

Between safe and infected
our words are banished behind a mask.
The first response is solitary.
I am sorry for the people of Wuhan
but a heavy dome has shut the doors
of travel, history, geography.
The borders are closing down,
there's no crossing the yellow barricades.

It was the Bat!
Here is a story of Covid-19,
a war of theory and blame.
Nothing is exempt:
Trade vessels, camels, caravans,
a palm civet, pangolins.
A wet market is scrubbed to death—
the sun is going down,
get ready, the wind is beginning to howl.

2

But it was us, I'm certain it was us—
Don't say it. The order is clear.
Don't say those things about greed and dominance,
about crossing the line,
fish, fowl, pelt; ivory, whalebone,
dispossession and theft.

Talk about our health.
It's a big deal—
Germ theory, Hazardous Material.
There's food and money on the table,
Live stream and Big Tech;
for the public good: Stay Home. Stay Safe.

3

How safe?
I woke up this morning trying to remember
the faces of my friends.
I have forgotten the shape of my slippers.
Is someone singing a song?
What is *song, touch—another country?*
Under surveillance
in plague condominiums, I am afraid
someone will get inside our heads.

After the war, the aftermath.
The sirens are blaring.
Someone is shouting:
I can't breathe!
And we are waiting,
shielding our dimming lamps.
Is the white mist spreading?

4

But we were born green. I am certain
in midsummer the Taan* will bloom again.
One day we will touch through the static
to honour the dead, wash the blood from our feet.
When there is nowhere to hide
between sheltered and homeless
the goal is the same—
to survive, to feel our hearts beating again.

5

To hell with hunger and despair!
In the labyrinth of life and death
if a second chance is the recovery of meaning,
a memory floating in our veins,

* Taan is a tall flowering tree believed to be protective and used for rituals to ward off evil.

there—beyond the grey city and red zones,
there lies my native village.
We'll carry the old and injured,
lift the children, lift them up high,
when the road finds us again, calling us to vital things
green in the sun.
Time is the wind carrying a big brush
mixing colours by ancient streams
flowing in all directions.

Pandemic; Another Lockdown

It is like digging through a narrow tunnel, on our knees with folded hands. The smell of bats is overpowering, hanging upside down in their mantle of sleep, dreaming past ages flickering with locusts and bees, and unknown life in a mysterious universe forever tilting between the hunter and the hunted, the victim and the host.

In the darkness an invisible bird is singing. Where is the sound coming from?

Maybe it is a rain bird, whistling for the clouds and the open sky.

Wonder of wonders! Perhaps there are parallel tunnels, a space for each one of us to find our way.

We are seeking a place of healing. We are looking for a second chance. Forget words that are false. The thin brittle words of false promises. We are only human. Find the word for mistake—error. Find the words to help us, fragile as we are, steeped in doubt, brutal because we are afraid, panic-stricken by a tiny wave, a whisper of mortality.

The way forward is to dig our way through.

What does it mean, to live on planet earth? A breathing in, a breathing out.

Through the tunnel, through the fumes of fungi and bacteria, we are crawling, aching, until our breath softens, limb and muscle learn to move in fluid unison. Our eyes begin to see in the dark. The silent trees are ablaze. The mountains are standing guard. The stars are looking at us. A white lily is nodding a lullaby.

After Gabo

No one can say it like you said it,
about love and magic,
solitude and growing old.

Here it's white butterflies
whirling around in the garden
and the scent of bitter almond
is the scent of orange blossom.

You know, love is a virus too,
jumping ship,
landing up in ports and cities
so eager, enchanted
by the banks of another river
in the time of quarantine.

There are lines and lines
of communication
jostling through a virtual pandemic,
a sadness named, unnamed.

Fermina Daza, is it true:
Everything is in our hands?

Outside my window
red hibiscus, red.
If the aim is to survive,
it's time to weigh anchor again.

For how long? Who knows.

Our old life is gone.
It's another summer
and the pages are turning
in a chronicle of things foretold.

One battered flag in a time of lockdown.
Despite contrary winds
a battered flag is fluttering,
you'll see it here and there
pointing in the direction of the future.
Salt water, caresses,
buoyant as the hearts of old lovers
young enough to believe
in forever.

Second Wave

Our fragility is no match for this second wave.
Again, this uproar of war and warriors.
On the ground, bullets and rocket attacks
in holy lands and streets of temple pagodas
among prophets and brothers—
who will protect the future, then?

All winter we lay buried with the dead.
Such a long night.
Alpha, Beta, Gamma, Delta,
virus variants without a country's name.
Again, we can't breathe.
In the heat of funeral pyres
someone is holding a lantern
standing over my head.
A word, poised on the tip of a blade;
have you found shelter yet?

Spring will arrive touching limbs and eyes.
Be still, yet.
Have you forgotten those fields and rivers
when a stone was a stone
born with its own soul?
The trees have their honour,

and men and women,
we are a celebration too,
writing letters
to remind each other that we live
alone, unknown, flawed, denied.
Hidden in our palms lies the future
born to return, life will lead us
rising from caves and cellars
with open hands.
We will find the summer again.

Narrative

I swallowed the current
At high tide I swam with the moon
I saw the wolves hunting
And all winter I dreamt of being a polar bear.

There are footprints climbing up to the sky,
And an ancient wing
Frozen beneath the earth.
Bone, teeth, hair, muscle,
There is food mingled in the swamp
And mangrove roots full of secrets.

The images mingle.
I see my father's face blind with age
Turned towards me with a smile of sweetness.
Bittersweet, unexpected.
What baffles me is the fleeting image,
Perhaps we matter in someone else's dream.

When There Are No More Words

When there are no more words,
the garrulous sentence is at last stripped to shreds,
into blood song, wreckage of bone,
the explosion of a wave
and ghost vessels dissolving
into this heart-cavity;
salt water.

So deep, this silence,
speechless with the mystery of your
absence.
Folded earth, folded,
dreaming of another horizon,
night wind drifting
into this heart-cavity;
breathless recall.

Long before we whirled into orbit
silence was a language.
In the amazing cadence of time—
one—two—three—four—
the deep hum of the universe,
infinite meaning
into this heart-cavity.
No writing on the wall.
No wall.

I'm Going Back to Old

I'm going back to old
To the springtime of water
And mesmerizing stories

Time, a silken rope
Summer night whispering illusion:

Is it true a stranger out of nowhere
Is better than a lover from the past?

Without a thought
Straight on with what is gone
Scattered jewels, melting ice
Beneath the clouds a silver road

This is no make-believe.
What does the moment know?
Rising on a bending wind
The shapeless moment before us
Is taking shape.

Sky. Mirror. Black earth.
Time. A songbird.
Those love songs were long
I'm going back to old.

The White Shirts of Summer

The afternoon sun burns, heart-stopping.
The movement of shadows is the length and stealth
of a cheetah.
Farewell to the room and the small fountain
that kept summer surging around us
now that the going is certain.

The dawn is pinned to my hair,
gust of sweet fragrance
lifting in the breeze.
Radiant, the white shirts of summer.

Without a map,
skimming over patches of land;
nothing was calculated.
Love was our prize, our sword,
our priceless amulet.
Your face in the cloud's rapture,
soft words, slow hands
and the light falling
white, on the white shirts of summer.

Slipping a knot, far from shore,
deep troughs of water.
Then we were bouncing high,
touching the moon.

Rivers of sand, grey mountains of the sea.
When moments vanish,
a finger of sun touches my face
closing the distance.
Salt white, oracle blue,
an ocean deep throws a wave,
knocking the boats in our hearts.
Forever, and forever—
radiant, the white shirts of summer.

The Oasis Is a Memory of Rain

The oasis is a memory of rain.
Beloved of the sun,
the long dune stretches dreaming a summer
in the playground of kings,
chasing a river with eyes and limbs
and the visage of a god.

Sometimes
beads of water float on the horizon.
The land is a master of disguise:
A burial place.
A mirage.
A resurrection.

A man turns into a date palm
nourished with dreams of rest and beauty.
Women lean against the wind
bending in ancient vigil
with the breath of sons and daughters,
oceans and continents,
tracing a memory—

through aeons,
breathing a garden, a lake,
to worship under the sky again

above the ruins of temples and tombs.
Lifting your gaze,
beloved of the sun, scented with rain,
crossing from darkness to light
over a bridge of bones.

Wishes

A big wind is whipping the garden.
Every night a thunderstorm wreaks havoc,
uprooting the jackfruit tree,
bending the wild palm and the electric pole,
destroying the garden lights.

Amidst the debris I think of wishes.
Maybe wishes keep us afloat.
I think of the man who was a doctor,
the old lady who thought she was self-sufficient,
the strong young man
who thought he would stay fit for long,
and the old man who wished for nothing
except to chant an old song
when memory swished by like a bright landscape.

People hang up wishes on the branches of trees.
They whisper to the wind
and hold a mirror to the moon.
Until one day,
after the boat on the high seas
and the craving for a storm,
a man retreats to a restful pond
holding but a single wish—
to find harbour in the simplicity of sunshine,
the patient shore, the arcing light of the sky.

Rain

Rain falling—
I'll catch you, says the tiger bamboo
shooting up straight as an arrow.
The China ducks stand still as priests
waiting.

The morning breeze is happy
releasing drops of water
whispering, the journey is not over.
Don't ache for love.
Someone will find the lost words.
Grow bamboo and yellow rose,
I'll find you again when I return.

Short Verse

Mountain

The future is the outline
of the mountain I gaze upon.
What is *beyond*?
Over the mountain
a glowing band of pink.
Spring clouds floating by.

***

In the streets of a town

Two young men get into an argument.
One of them pulls out a gun and shoots the other dead.
A bitter wind is choking us. Beautiful words drift past.
A scent of summer, those days of love and longing,
such fragility.
Folded wings. Be still, my heart.

***

A pause in the rain

Through the dark clouds a blue window
floating above the storm.
Life-pumping heart canvas
stretched taut for a brushstroke.
Yellow sun. Bright wings.

***

There is a street with a shop of maps

Perhaps a meeting will happen,
in a market of lamps or on a sloping hillside.
Here we are, still remembering.

***

A storm is brewing

The wind is blowing in from all directions.
Chinar tree, tilting north, going home.

***

Muse

If I lived near the sea
how would the mornings have been
waking up?
Would I have watched for that dragon boat
rising on the horizon; or watched the gulls
flying salt lines in the air,
written another love poem
making waves?

Across the wild bay ancient cities are calling
resounding with history, men and metal,
armour, ships,
a smouldering fire
burning in the libraries of time.
If we had turned that way,
stepping on a stone bridge,
another poem might have been inscribed
with our names
on the old walls of moon and stars.

Domes and minarets. Terracotta.
A flowering almond in the garden we left behind,
and fountains gushing water
out of stone lips, feeding Calla lilies.

If I live in the mountains
the days are the same.
Breathing in the slow mist,
slow arrangement of possibilities—
the river imagines it will meet the sea,
that piece of mountain,
drops of water from a stream
beating in our hearts, floating in our veins.
Pray it is buoyant.

Sun

(Donyi-polo)

When they say time heals
it means time can transform memory—
what someone chooses to remember, that is.
And when you sit in the sun, remembering,
your heart is the centre of the world.
It is the sun.
Particles, moments, memories—
specks flying in space
revolving around this sun.
And you can arrange light and shadow,
soften blows, stretch, pull, tug.
Obliterate mistakes, obliterate regret.

But the sun is the sun.
The sun knows.
Better to be honest.
We'll see about the rest.

Folklore

The coming of death

Since the coming of death
tears blind our eyes when we bury the dead.
This salt was given
with a handful of earth from a hornet
weeping over the grave of her children,
mixed with the sweet song of a bird
weeping after a storm broke her nest.

Tears—
This must be the path of tears
saying what cannot be told,
pouring our love on a land
lying so beautiful in drapes and folds
offering love, sleep, rest.
Today, tomorrow: shining, contained,
moulded in a drop to show us
the truth of who we are.
Our hearts were never made of stone.

***

Finding the way

We ate the words. We were hungry.
We ate the words.

In the cave of our ancestors
we drank the wine of ritual,
sprinkled blood on the ground.
Who knows if it rained or snowed,
entangled in a myth
finding the way was hard
when we swallowed the sunrise and the sunset.

All the words were eaten.
What were the words, what was written?

In a dream the great hunter made a speech.
Come, he said, let us leave this torment of darkness
water and mist,
and sing for the river flowing east.
Undying on the wild way we followed
carrying the wind and waters,
the flying sky,
and the stag on the horizon
dancing among the stars.

Tomorrow—
Would we reach tomorrow?
From the cave of our ancestors

the void continues to fill.
The letters of earth and sky
written in the outline of the hills:
A sun-seed in the backbone,
the tenacity of grass;
root strength
and the fragrance of fleeting things,
the purpose of growing corn
and living mud
feeding breath with fire and bones
in the silence of our hills,
the fury of our skies.

***

The hour of freedom

I went to the forest to find the hidden arrow,
the arrow straight as a sunbeam.
With this I would be armed for life.

Who stole my child?
Who placed this sadness of stolen colours
in the shelter of my lap?

The wild trees sprang up.
The mountain stepped back.
For a thousand years I dragged a net
sieving debris clinging to the depths of water,
watching the night tangled with the dawn.

Who will inherit tomorrow?
Hell is a closed door denying us
the shelter of words and meaning.

The word, when it was first uttered, meant everything.
A spark fanned by the wing of sky
breaking the shape of silence
into a heartbeat, song, hope.
Most of all, hope—
to want what we want, even though it was a falling
into the hard road of angels and demons
and the intoxication of fire.

There are barriers between the living and the dead.
Sometimes the veil is transparent.
One day we will recognize each other again
there, my friend with the ready smile, the quiet face,
the mystery of your presence granting hope, illumination.
The land speaks to us when we are grieving:

Past present future, the holy bundle of three.
Earth sky water.
I will restore the life of your failing pulse,
hold your hand, and teach you to bear grief.

Tears—
This must be the path of tears,
this ebb and flow tugging at my heart
filling up with salt. A few saline drops
mixed in the ageless churning of the waters.

Across the sky smoke is billowing,
a flower falls on an old gravestone.
The hornets are tearing their hearts
burning in the yellow sun.
A bird sits on my shoulder, weeping.
A song of flying is floating over the valley.

***

Innocent Danger

This poem draws from Arunachal folklore about snakes and man. Snakes once wore beads, then man snatched them, and the species have been bitter enemies ever since. The title of the poem is taken from an interview with Rom Whitaker, 'A Life Less Ordinary,' in Round Glass Sustain (roundglasssustain.com).

My grandfather said:
Wear your beads.
I'll give you a tongue lashing
if you lose your inheritance.
Red, yellow, black, white.
Once upon a time we wore beads.

Brothers and friends
with the salt crab, tiger and bear,
until we met the sons of Tani*
chasing a bead thief. They said:
'Guilty or not!'
And so, one day long ago
we were deprived of our beads.

Elder brother lost his fangs.
Cursed with flies and hornets
into a pit of loathing, we survived

---

* Tani is the Adi word for Man.

to dwell in other worlds,
climbing to the sky in a map of stars
curled around an ancient staff
in a symbol of healing.

No one remembers.
But I remember what happened to us,
faced with extinction
in the inscrutable moment
of a sudden encounter.
Pay heed—
venom is a bitter drop
triggered by the memory
of our lost beads.

There are places where we thrive.
In Leporiang we met a man,
not sinister,
his eyes aglow with wonder,
asking: What is *Barta?*
The wise ones would say:
'One of us! One of us!
There is no other.'

If you remember, we were a symphony
of life and minstrels together.
In the garden of time
the crocodile carries the sun,
sailing free under Polaris
the wandering turtle wanders
playing his flute.

Whale Shark

Trust is a gift
Even though a brutal blow
May end your life.
Trust is a gift, but
Whale shark
Never let us know where you go.

Trust is the gift
That sways you in the deep
Moving close to men and boats
Gulping light and water
Big as an island
Your breath parts the waters

A vision of rare beauty
If you survive this encounter—
The frenzy of saviours, scientists, do-gooders
Even entranced, awestruck me.
Whale shark, never yield your secrets
Slide away, plummet down
to your secret continents
Never let us know where you go.

Weather Report

I love the way bamboo burns
entering into a quiet relationship
with air and light.
The clouds are spreading,
black gills sprouting over the mountain.
A frothing sound—
Here comes the rain!
Sliding down the green stem,
flooding the rice fields.

We cross-check the Met reports:
Dry in Delhi, unnatural floods across Europe,
high winds, heat in Alaska.
The earth is drifting with trade winds,
who knows what will happen.

Beneath the oceans a mile-wide current
circles the continents
speaking a language spoken since birth.
Time, say it. A measure of understanding.
Time, say it. A measure of love.
The desire of clouds in the burning air—
More rain for the North eastern states of India!

Rain Words

I say: rain words.
But today is dry.
We just talk about the weather
our words crackling like bone
rigid with time,
as if we were living in a desert.

What we felt yesterday
has fallen asleep.
So quietly, surreptitiously, the moments
have been standing around us
building up to this dream of forgetfulness.
Is that yesterday?

Leaves and thorns, buds and sweet scent
everything is waiting.
On the night of the staring fish moon
Time is a ghost from the past,
the air in search of a voice.
Rain words, bone words.
A murmur of possibilities.

A Brief Walk in the Mountains

1

Rush of water, snow and berries.
The voices of children
shouting across the valley.

2

The tiger's footprint vanishes.
The jungle road is empty,
with no sign of miracles.

3

The sea with eyes and arms.
Mindfulness
like an octopus.

4

The night is cold and high.
The outline of a poem
is creeping up the hill.

5

Memory is colour.
The pages turn. In my heart
a lingering flame tree.

Full Moon

It's a full moon night.
Across the world
all my friends are smiling,
making love with words and letters
to one another,
and to fabulous strangers
who are also travellers
sharing limb and eyes,
tugging at Orion's belt,
pulling at the bow,
shooting into the distance.

Simulacrum

Summer trees under a grey sky.
Is the sky pretending to weep?
Are we pretending to be busy
digging black earth, planting roots?

Leaning against a tree
a man turns into a seed
stealing mud, water, moonlight.
A sign of life is the flutter of wings.

Beauty. Grace. Wit.
Today I am wary of words.
The red flower on a tree
is a visage of longing,
a virus hidden in the scent of spring.

Don't forget the words of stones, asking:
What is not real?
Everything jostles into new space.
No messages. No lessons learnt.

In the changing emblem of meaning,
the emptiness is a road

opening in all directions.
Circle of sunlight, breath of leaves,
knowing nothing of journeys
we become our longing,
in silent fervour
shedding our skin in the sun.

February

Coral tree. Silk cotton.
The conical hills are laughing.
One black heron.

Ginger

My desk is full of ginger.
In a hurry spilled among papers and pen,
a clock, notebooks,
the shoots of ginger are pink,
unloaded here for planting.

Without a word,
never minding my books and letters,
ready to stand on their own.

Ready earth, ready soil,
ready summer warmth
and tender rain.
Ready season
whispering the green alphabets
of time.

Music Concert

The vibrant art of musicians
Singing birds to life,
And the giant shadow of a tree
On the mud wall, dancing.

A group of seventeen,
Six, six, five,
A woman is singing the desert
Into a storm.
The old men are knitting the air with music,
Knitting music out of the air.
A sob, a wail, wingbeat
and the meaning of crescendo,
Nothing more than an exchange of glances
And waves rising in my heart.
And nothing more than my heart,
In my hands, clapping.

This Weather Would Have Suited You

A soft, whispering rain
Tentative, shadowy.
One big drop on the tin roof—
TOCK!

I always thought this weather would have suited you.
Shining leaves, earth scent,
The scarf on your head draping the moment
In celebration with seed and soil, planting boats
To ferry us into the territories of the future.

What did we know?
Nothing.

The bright comet comes into orbit, and disappears.
Some things are over, done with,
Once and for all.
The eclipse passes,
Earth's shadow falling away into space.
Is the universe finished?

Time is a scattering, claiming its share.
One by one the alphabets are returning,
The big and the small,

Arriving like birds and the branches of trees,
Arriving with news—
The rain that falls, harder,
The fire that burns, brighter.
Like destiny revealed on a full moon night
Telling us of love and decay
To become a story
Born from the gardens of the sky.

Family Sciuridae

The beauty of the Lipo is stunning.
Soft, grey fur. Turn him over—
red-smeared sun
spread on his belly.

I do not know how to pay tribute
to this presence,
this antiquity of colour.
The universe opens in boxes,
small windows of glowing life
so perfect, each in its element.

Champion messenger, entering all worlds
even in death, in unison with men and women.
To fly, glide, fall with grace,
with no sense of passing.

The flying squirrel has the teeth of a rodent,
lower incisors long and curved upwards.
Big eyes. Delicate ankles and feet.
I wish I could stroke it back to life.

It has the most horrific cry, they say.
If you hear him, you will be
frightened out of your wits.
A blood-curdling half-human otherworldly cry—
Why not? It likes to shriek.

Disguise

Who would have thought
The tadpole born in a lily pond
Would drown the rain
With the chorus of frogs?

Lost in thought
The river drowns us.
Language, speech, desire
Waiting to be born.

Floating Island

The sloping mountain is trying to reach me
stretching down into the water.
Dear one, don't go away,
rest, rest on my shoulder.

In the floating darkness a woman is asleep
pressing her cheek on my pillow
vivid with dreams.
The birds of summer are nesting in her breast.

Who knows which way the spinning current will spin—
Farewell, blind mountain, pasted on the sky.
When the day is folded away
my heart clings to the life of water—

Into the deep, into the sea green
navigating on a heartbeat.
The lilies are shooting up like swordfish
and the woman is laughing, laughing.

The Sorrow of Women

They are talking about hunger.
They are saying
there is an unquenchable fire
burning in our hearts.
My love, what shall I do?
I am thinking how I may lose you
to war, and big issues
more important than me.

Life is so hard like this.
Nobody knows why.
It is like fire,
it is like rainwater, sand, glass.
What will I do, my love,
if my reflection disappears?

They are talking about a place
where rice flows in the streets,
about a place where there is gold
in the leaves of trees.
They are talking about displacement
when the opium poppy was growing,
dizzy in the sun,
happy in a state of believing.

And they are talking about escape,
about liberty, men and guns.
Ah! The urgency for survival.
But what will they do,
not knowing the sorrow of women?

A Death

The winter was long. We made many sacrifices. Early this morning a young boy died.

Was he ill? Was it his heart? Was it drugs?

'He helped me wash the dishes,' his mother said. 'He had mended his ways.' She had waited for him to wake up. Death, she said, came like a thief and stole him away from her. Now he was gone.

What are the words to say to the living? High on the hill, the prayer flags are fluttering without a sound.

Pray, do not let death enter this house.

Gone

We have long journeys in our blood.
The road has no end.
The lanes and streets are lined in my eyes,
the horizon burns in my head.
At night we sleep with guns and gulls
tugging at land and oceans,
and ropes coiled to barren rock
where once flowers were to seed
pumping blood and singing voices.

How would anyone know what we have tried to do—
when there was me, and you,
and there was the burnt black hill
monumental with the faces of our people,
until the next moonrise showed us
something about change
and the existence of dreams.

The steep hillside is a hard place.
There is nowhere to rest our feet
even when I want to kneel and pray,
moved to tears by a rainbow sky.

What is felt,
left unsaid
is a sadness.

Bereft of our symbols
this strange tattoo in my heart
is the sound of footsteps.

I know the clouds are hiding behind your eyes
even as you kiss my brow,
but this is the way that was promised us
the day we met ten thousand messengers
carrying the whispers of the world.

Love Song of the Warrior

He returns with light and life like a rushing wind
filling all space,
and turning in the warmth of oceans and streams
in a yearning of patience, he buries his arrows at last
and weeps into the earth.

This path is treacherous.
It turns friend to foe
and wolves follow, like fixed shadows, always,
darkening my heart.

I blended a love once of red fruit and bitter herb;
and tender voices and shining eyes
bore me a necklace of blessings
crafted, once, in a shrine of light.

This first spear was gentle.
It bled my heart in strange dizziness;
an unknown sensation filled my blood
driving me fearless into the night;
one by one my beads slipped away
like vivid moments obscured by time.

Then blend me again the darkness and light,
the white rose and bitter root
when life subsides and dark shadows follow
like ancient sorrows obstructing the stars.

This spear will be sharp.
I see the terror in these eyes;
obstacle of tears.

At great risk we tasted the happiness of earth;
tender voices and shining eyes
crafted once in a shrine of light.

Before the failing wick, the flashing river runs
like tenderness and belief, breaking all barriers...

In the stream of my blood, memory hums
softly, telling me
near death and the broken summer
as long as I remember, we live.

Stay with the Song

The afternoon belongs to the dove
weeping for her fall from heaven.*
The feast of life is laid before our eyes,
but the ticking moment
discloses nothing about time;
its footsteps, and their meaning.
Evening—
The sun goes away
carrying its quiver of arrows.
Every word we utter now is a memory
until the sun returns.
Stay with the song.
All night—
Don't lose the chord
that binds all things together.
Rain blows down from the hills
pushed by grey clouds,
and a white, ordinary moon
suddenly draws our gaze upwards.

* In Adi mythology the dove once lived with the sun and carried her baby while the sun travelled across the sky. One day the carrying strap fell down to earth. The dove flew down to retrieve it but could not return to heaven. That is why, it is believed, the dove weeps.

Daybreak—
The bright cry of the peacock.
Morning light touches the grass.
It is time to leave.
Not all the things we know will heal us.
Not all the things we fear will kill us.

The River

Do not stay too long by the river.
The river is a wayward god.
It is an elephant, a lion;
sometimes they call it a horse.
One summer we thought it was a peacock
turning in the yellow dust
that filled our eyes with gold.

I saw a woman floating in a lily pond,
in a mountain of mist, wrapped in a cloud
streaming with tendrils and pollen dust.

I thought: the river is a woman,
a country, a name,
a note of music trapped in the white current,
a sheet of paper carrying a secret map.
The skyline is where it begins
between the darkness and the summit,
in the birthplace of thirst.

Do not stay too long by the river.
It is a drowning spirit,
a strong-armed god,
drawing and withdrawing such seasons;
flowing river, standing still,
river sea, river ocean,
river of all our summers
collecting the salt of our lives.

Man and Brother*

I go where the forest is unknown.
Under the sacred tree I'll place my bow,
the night will be long,
the wild birds are restless,
but I'll wear my disguise
and wait.

Green intoxication
fading swiftly into darkness.
Alone I wait, wearing my amulet,
waiting, where I can hear best
instructions from my ancestors.

A footstep.
Silence.
The first drop of rain
breaks a leaf.
Footsteps.
Silence.
A twig breaks
and thunder raises the canopy
of trees.

* This is with reference to the belief that man and tiger were born brothers. The killing of a tiger is equivalent to killing a man and the rituals associated with a tiger hunt are rigorous.

The tiger runs swiftly from my father's house
calling my name:
Brother, Man brother!
Have mercy for our destiny!

The long dream strikes from the past.
Too late, I answer.
The gods decide my luck is futile,
perhaps the propitiation was mistaken.
This time, this time,
death is a red flower breaking over my heart.

Grieving, my village will be grieving.
For five days they will honour restraint
then search the night again
for compensation.

Run swiftly then, my brother.
Oh, my brother,
have mercy for our destiny!

Man and Brother (2)

Before the day is over, one kill, and the deed is done.
The alert faces are speckled, beads of sweat on the ground,
the sun is drooping over the hill when the last wild tiger is killed
and a heartbeat like thunder echoes from earth to sky.
Deep into the night the women tell stories.
In the incestuous hunger of birth and creation, they say,
we tumbled down the same stairway
of stars, fire and salt.
All the zodiac was given to us;
signs, symbols, the marks of destiny,
choreography of blood
frame by frame—a life!
But now the red mantle* is being folded away.

When the moon rises the hill will be empty.
Perhaps a long silhouette will lope across the sky line,
but it will only be a silhouette;
all the fire remaining in our hearts
will melt like ice and dead bone
until a brother cries out again,
seeking a brother's lost face.

* A hunter who had killed a tiger was received at the village gate by women carrying a red ga-lè (wrap skirt of Adi women) to shield the hunter from the eyes of the slain tiger.

Without his footprint we would not know how to be brave.
Alone with the wind, perhaps a sigh will save us now—
Burning, incandescent memory
of the swift stream and forest light;
when somewhere, in his sleep, a child whimpers
dreaming a dream of an ancestor
calling him back, calling him back,
to the striped summer of the tiger.

Prayer Flags

Like delicate tracery
you mapped the delusions of my heart,
planning the evening, and the rain.
It was revenge, and I did not know,
not recognising your art.

We speak of rebirth,
the cycle of life and death;
but words are faithless—
I ask you again:
Who prays to the wild wind,
who cries to the first sky—
You bring me pain,
Oh! You bring me pain!

We should have known
life's little madness would find us again.
Keeper of the holy mountain,
facing the four heavens,
the art of healing is slow with doubt
but all life is turning in shadow image—

Now my cup is empty.
I only know
the sun and moon
crown the heart of the blade.

Prayer Flags (2)

The wet mountain road.
This is where we spent all our time
wondering if we would get across.

Someone planted a prayer flag in my heart.
Green living, yellow earth,
white clouds, and juniper incense
mingled with the blue left by a sea
that once owned this land.

Perhaps the storm will blow it down
someday,
after it has halted the wind
a thousand times.

We found each other yesterday,
when they told us the past is over.
Now we are floating smudges of colour
flying high
over the mountain barrier.

Remembrance

Why did we think it was trivial
that it would rain every summer,
that nights would be still with sleep
and that the green fern would uncurl
ceaselessly by the roadside?

Why did we think survival was simple,
that river and field would stand forever,
invulnerable even to the dreams of strangers?
For we knew where the sun lay resting
in the folded silence of the hills.

This summer it rains more than ever.
The footfall of soldiers is drowned and scattered.
In the hidden exchange of news we hear
that weapons are multiplying in the forest.

The jungle is a big eater,
hiding terror in the carnivorous green.

Why did we think ritual gods would survive
deathless in memory,
in trees and stones and the sleep of babies?
Now, when we close our eyes
and cease to believe, god dies.

For as long as remembrance
men stared at fire and water.
We dwell in the mountains and do not know
what the world hears about us.

Foragers for a destiny,
all the days of our lives
we stare at the outline of the hills,
lifting our eyes to the invincible sky.

No Dreams

The days are nothing.
Plant and foliage grow silently,
at night a star falls down,
a leopard leaves its footprints.

The wind blows into my eyes.
Sometimes it stirs my heart
to see the land so plain and beautiful.

If I sit very still
I think I can join the big mountains
in their speechless ardour.

Where no sun is visible
the hills are washed with light.
The river sings,
love floats!
Love floats!
But I have no dreams.

Small Towns and the River

Small towns always remind me of death.
My hometown lies calmly amidst the trees,
it is always the same,
in the summer or winter
with the dust flying
or the wind howling down the gorge.

Just the other day someone died.
In the dreadful silence we wept
looking at the sad wreath of tuber rose.
Life and death, life and death.
Only the rituals are permanent.

The river has a soul.
In the summer it cuts through the land
like a torrent of grief. Sometimes,
sometimes, I think it holds its breath
seeking the land of fish and stars.

The river has a soul.
It knows, stretching past the town,
from the first drop of rain to dry earth
and mist on the mountaintops,
the river knows
the immortality of water.

A shrine of happy pictures
marks the days of childhood.
Small towns grow with anxiety
for future generations.
The dead are placed pointing west.
When the soul rises
it will walk into the golden east,
into the house of the sun.

In the cool bamboo,
restored in the sunlight,
life matters, like this.

In small towns by the river
we all want to walk with the gods.

Jingles

The slow sun of Itanagar hangs over us.
The summer breeds cicadas,
in a trance the evening descends
like mad castanets drowning the iron land.

Come dancing, says the radio.
There, a pine-tree cloud hangs over the moon.

In the dance halls we were only fragrance and motion.
No sound disturbed. No face threatened.
We did not know possession.
Now the lights of the town stare bitterly in my direction.
Too late for tears or hate,
dare I laugh?

Come dancing, says the radio.
From this moment to the next there will be
more losers and fighters wintering in silence.

The wind blows. The crooner croons.
The dry lips of winter drive the weightless leaves.
People you love disappear.
You go away, they cease to exist.
Why should I shrink myself to fit?

Come dancing, says the radio.
Distance lends ease.
I bury my heart under a cloud
and wait for a strong wind.

Who knows about such matters?
Is it a star, or a fish?
Along the rutted road we go, my love and I,
rutted road to nowhere
in the glittering dark,
bamboo whispering bamboo talk
and martial art in my heart.

The hills will fall down.
There will be new rivers.
Tomorrow the leaves and trees will shine again,
and all the people of the town will look
strange and wonderful.

Let No Tear*

Let no tear touch you now.
Travellers look at one another
and cannot tell who is going where, why.
The crossing is sudden
from brief reverie to this welt of pain.

There were no voices
when the journey began.
Facing the slow descent
from streets of stone
perhaps you signalled, fiercely mute,
now the dry river swells,
turning all blame into fiercer regret.

How shall we move?
In the way of tradition,
ritual and blessing,
with no tear to touch you now,
the women will return to tell the stories,
the men will sit by you, strengthening,
strengthening ties and talking.

---

* Songs of lamentation, called *penges*, recalling childhood and youth are sung in impromptu verse during funeral rites.

Quiet and cleansed
into that land of light we'll bid you move;
a mother's gaze embracing all grief
will kindle the chanting;

when the singing rises
death itself will cease.
Blue beads* in your hair will turn you
a boy again, whirling
the wild mountains to sleep.

* Among the Adi it is customary to fasten beads and sacred twine to the hair and wrist of relatives of the deceased.

Time

In time we come to know it all,
the sleeping idiot
and the truth he tells,
the callous words,
the stinging waves
and the sudden about turn.

We have seen mountains,
cities of ships, desert waste
and fertile islands,
and in the half-sleep
we have heard
the gnashing of teeth
and nightmares of lions.

Children have grown
plump, and sleepy eyed
then thinned in the distance,
shaped with veins of steel.

In time we come to know it all.
The laughing mouth,
the sculptured hand,
the damp of flesh and fur,
the awakening terror
of loneliness.

Stone Lions

Soft snow faces glisten
on the lion's back.
After the turning of the wheel
the stillness of the form;
and I thought
I would never be afraid again.

Birthplace

We are the children of the rain,
of the cloud woman,
brother to the stone and bat.
In our cradle of bamboo and vine,
in our long houses we slept,
and when morning came
we were refreshed.

There were no strangers
in our valley.
Recognition was instant
as clan by clan we grew,
and destiny was simple,
like a green shoot
following direction
like the sun and moon.

The first drop of water
gave birth to man.
From red sheath
to green stem
and the spreading wind.

We descend
from solitude and miracles.

ALSO FROM SPEAKING TIGER

ESCAPING THE LAND

Mamang Dai

Combining history, myth and contemporary politics, *Escaping the Land* is a saga of a beautiful but sometimes turbulent land and its people. Acclaimed poet-novelist Mamang Dai takes us on an unforgettable journey from the land of Kojum-Koja, a sacred place beyond time, to the formation of the modern state of Arunachal Pradesh.

Maying, a woman who has lived away from the state, returns in order to write a history of the people who have shaped her land. As she speaks to them and leafs through old records, a myriad stories and destinies unfold—an ancient flood and a lake full of stars; conflict and curiosity that led to the establishment of NEFA (North-East Frontier Agency); hardy men and women, like Lipun, who walked the highest mountain passes to establish connections with remote tribes; the 'rainman', who can read the elements because he is so closely tied to them; and Lutor, the shaman's child, who can feel the pulse of his people, even when he is disillusioned with public life.

But there are also land and forest mafia, corrupt politicians in cahoots with violent militants, and friends who can turn foes to satisfy their ambitions. Maying recoils from the murky theatre of the modern state, but realizes, too, that 'our hearts are taken, given, lost' but 'what is never lost is the original obsession that was a dream of love'.

Lyrical, vital and epic in scale, *Escaping the Land* is the story of a people and a place that is, like the best novels, the story of all humanity.